PLATYPUS

This edition first published in the United States in 1997 by
MONDO Publishing

By arrangement with MULTIMEDIA INTERNATIONAL (UK) LTD

The publisher would like to thank Les Peach, Platypus Keeper,
Royal Melbourne Zoo, Australia, for his assistance.
Pie Diagrams p. 15 by Dominic Fanning, reference for diagram p. 11, and reference for
illustration p. 13, all from The Platypus by Tom Grant, NSW University Press, Australia, 1984.
Photograph Credits: Peter Marsack/Lochman Transparencies: front cover;
Jack Green: all interior photographs.
Text copyright © 1987 by Joan Short, Jack Green, and Bettina Bird
Illustrations copyright © 1987 by Andrew Wichlinski

For information contact:
MONDO Publishing
980 Avenue of the Americas • New York, New York 10018
Visit our website at www.mondopub.com

Printed in China
First Mondo printing, October 1996
08 09 10 11 12   11 10 9 8

Originally published in Australia in 1987 by Horwitz Publications Pty Ltd
Original development by Robert Andersen & Associates and Snowball Educational
Designed by Brash Design   Cover redesign by Charlotte Staub

Library of Congress Cataloging-in-Publication Data
Short, Joan.
   Platypus / by Joan Short, Jack Green, and Bettina Bird ; illustrated by
Andrew Wichlinski.
      p.   cm. — (Mondo animals)
   Includes index.
   Summary: Introduces the physical characteristics, habits, and natural
environment of the platypus, an animal found only in Australia.
      ISBN 1-57255-195-X (pbk. : alk. paper)
      1. Platypus—Juvenile literature. [1. Platypus.] I. Green, Jack. II. Bird,
   Bettina. III. Wichlinski, Andrew, ill. IV. Title. V. Series.
   QL737.M72S48   1996
   599.1—dc20   96-15299
                                                                      CIP
                                                                       AC

Cover: Australian Platypus

PLATYPUS

by Joan Short, Jack Green, and Bettina Bird

Illustrated by Andrew Wichlinski

Contents

This photograph taken by Jack Green is believed to be a rare shot of the platypus with its eyes open under water.

Introduction

The platypus is a fascinating animal, found only in Australia. It inhabits freshwater rivers and lakes where it swims, feeds, and digs burrows. It has a most unusual lifestyle.

1 Physical Features

The platypus has a number of unique features. It is the only animal in the world to have a bill, webbed feet, and fur, and to feed in water.

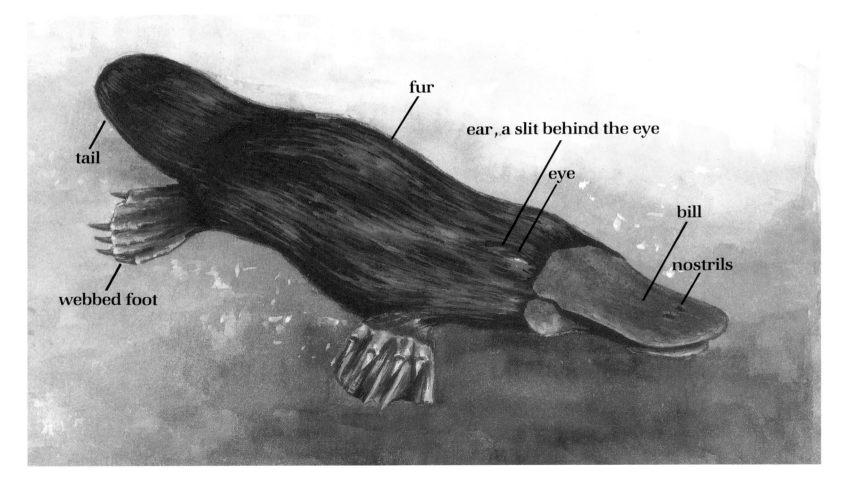

fur

ear, a slit behind the eye

eye

bill

nostrils

tail

webbed foot

Feet

The feet of the platypus are designed for both swimming and digging. The webbing between its claws enables it to swim with ease. When the platypus is digging, the webbing tucks safely away so that it cannot be damaged and so that it does not interfere with the platypus's movement.

Breathing

The platypus swims under water but it cannot breathe under water. It swims to the surface to breathe air through nostrils at the front of its bill. It can stay under water for 2 to 8 minutes, depending on how active it is.

foot with webbing extended for swimming

foot with webbing tucked away for digging

The Male Platypus

The average male platypus grows to about 20 inches (50.8 centimeters) long. It has a hollow spur behind each hind leg which is connected to a venom gland in the thigh. Some scientists think that these spurs may be used to protect the platypus from predators, but there is no proof of this.

The Female Platypus

The average female platypus is smaller than the male, growing to about 17 inches (43.2 centimeters) long. The young female platypus also has spurs on its hind legs but it loses them when it is 8 to 10 months old. The female platypus does not have a pouch to carry its young. It lays eggs in a nest and feeds its young on milk once they have hatched. This milk is secreted through pores on the belly and is licked up by the babies.

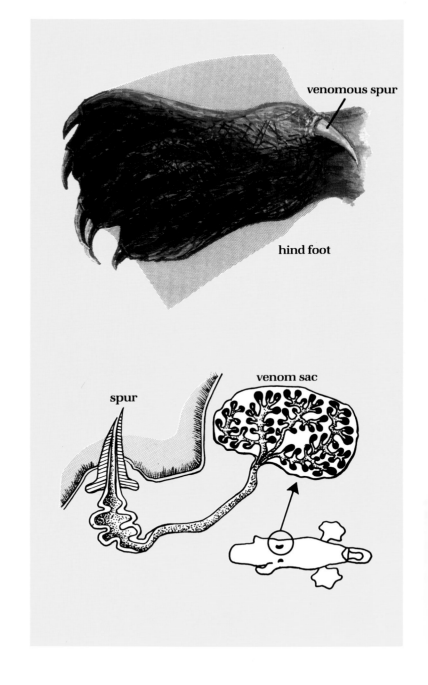

venomous spur

hind foot

venom sac

spur

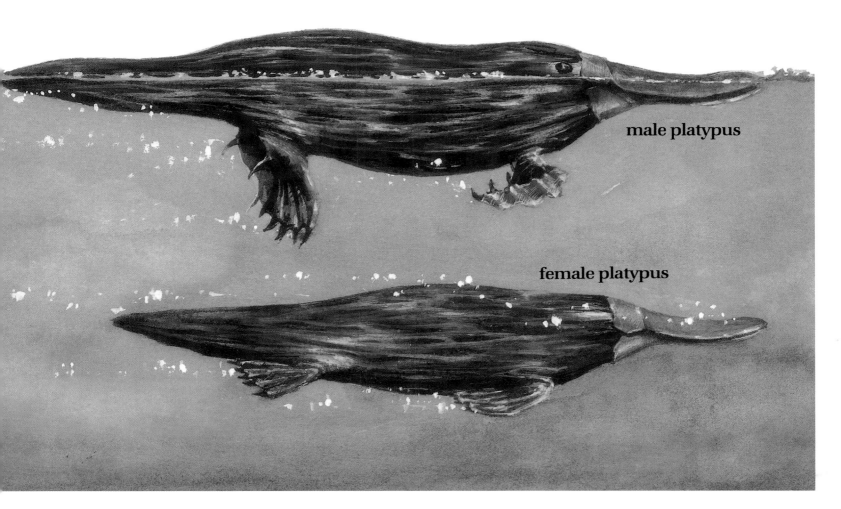

male platypus

female platypus

2 Habitat

The platypus lives in both hot and cold climates. It inhabits freshwater creeks, rivers, and lakes in eastern Australia from Cooktown, in north Queensland, all the way south to Tasmania.

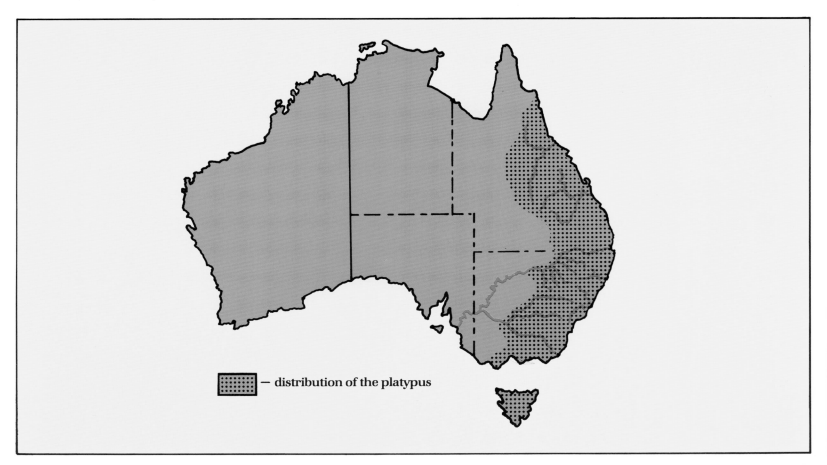

▓▓▓ — distribution of the platypus

The Burrow and Sleeping Chamber

The platypus digs a burrow in the banks of the creek, river, or lake where it lives.

The burrow may be from 20 to 52 feet (6 to 16 meters) long. At the end is a sleeping chamber. There are often several entrances above water level. Entrances are well hidden from predators by overhanging reeds, grass, and bushes.

The burrow is usually a tight fit. As the platypus forces its way inside, any water in its fur is squeezed out. The animal enters the sleeping chamber reasonably dry.

3 Food

Feeding Times

The platypus usually feeds in the early hours of the morning and from late afternoon into the night. In between feeding times it rests in its burrow or lies in the sun at the burrow entrance.

Finding Food

The platypus finds all of its food in the water. When it is feeding it moves its head from side to side so that the sensitive nerves in its bill can find the food.

Diet

The platypus eats crayfish, worms, insects, fish eggs, and water plants. It also takes in mud from the river bed as it probes with its bill. The mud contains tiny water creatures called plankton, which are probably also part of its diet.

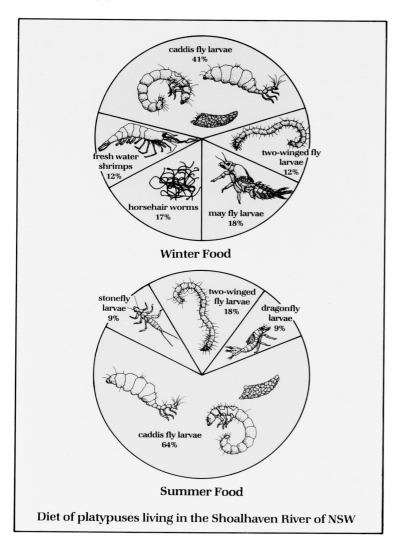

Winter Food

Summer Food

Diet of platypuses living in the Shoalhaven River of NSW

Feeding

When the platypus has found its food it comes up to the surface to breathe and to chew the food. It crushes its food with horny grinding pads at the base of its bill.

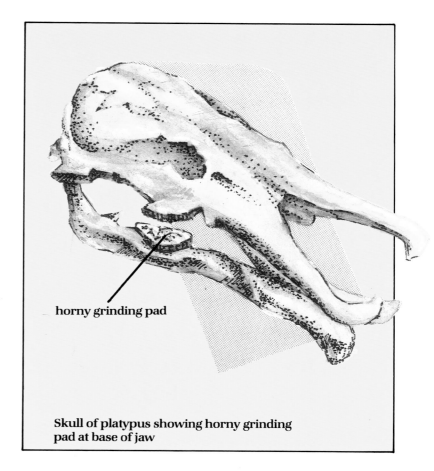

horny grinding pad

Skull of platypus showing horny grinding pad at base of jaw

4 Reproduction

Mating

Scientists think that platypuses mate in the water some time between July and November. Mating time depends on the climate in which the platypuses live.

Building the Nesting Chamber

The female is ready to lay her eggs about four weeks after mating. She digs a special burrow branching off the main burrow, and at the end of this new burrow she digs a nesting chamber. She collects leaves and grass and builds her nest. She also collects a wad of mud and damp leaves. She brings this into the burrow and uses her tail to push it all together to block the entrance.

Laying the Eggs

The female platypus usually lays two eggs. However, sometimes she lays only one, or as many as three. When the eggs are laid the platypus curls herself around them to keep them warm. The mud and leaves blocking the entrance help to keep the air moist. This stops the leathery eggs from drying out.

Incubation

While she is incubating her eggs the female platypus does not leave her burrow to feed. Her body lives on the fat stored in her tail during the ten days required for the eggs to hatch. The entrance to the burrow is blocked all this time so there is less and less oxygen left in the air inside the burrow. Scientists think that the platypus has a special way of storing oxygen in its blood to last through incubation.

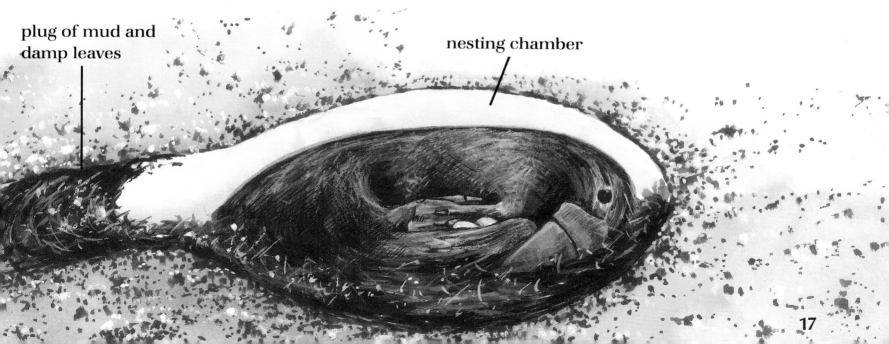

plug of mud and damp leaves

nesting chamber

The Baby Platypus

A baby platypus uses a tooth to break out of its egg. The tooth falls off soon afterwards. The baby platypus is about ½ inch (15 millimeters) long. Its bill is short, soft, and slightly fleshy around the edges so that it can suck milk from the milk patches on its mother's belly. The mother needs food to replenish her milk so she hurries out of her burrow from time to time, feeds quickly, then returns.

young, suckling

The eyes of the baby platypus do not open until it is about 11 weeks old. A week later it takes short swims close to the entrance of the burrow and begins to search for its own food. It growls, squeaks, and plays like a puppy. After 3 months it is fully weaned and able to look after itself.

young platypuses at play

5 Safeguarding the Platypus

Protection

Many years ago hunters killed the platypus for its fur. People feared that the platypus would become extinct because it was being killed in such large numbers. State governments then passed laws to protect the platypus. This means that nobody is allowed to kill or capture a platypus. Anyone found doing so can be fined or even sent to jail.

Preserving the Habitat of the Platypus

Today naturalists are sure that many thousands of platypuses are living in the secluded creeks, rivers, and lakes of their natural habitat. However, protecting the platypus by law may not be enough to make sure it survives. It is also important that the places where the platypus lives be kept in their natural state. If too many rivers are dammed and too many secluded creeks are turned into cement-lined canals, the natural habitat of the platypus will be destroyed forever. If this happens the platypus cannot possibly survive.

typical habitat of the platypus

Index